THE BABES IN THE WOOD

 Grolier Educational Corporation

SORE SICKE THEY WERE
AND LIKE TO DYE

THE BABES IN THE WOOD

NOW ponder well, you parents deare,
These wordes which I shall write;
A doleful story you shall heare,
In time brought forth to light.

A gentleman of good account
In Norfolke dwelt of late,
Who did in honour far surmount
Most men of his estate.

Sore sicke he was, and like to dye,
No helpe his life could save;
His wife by him as sicke did lye,
And both possest one grave.

No love between these two was lost,
    Each was to other kinde;
In love they liv'd, in love they dyed,
    And left two babes behinde:

The one a fine and pretty boy,
    Not passing three yeares olde;
The other a girl more young than he,
    And fram'd in beautye's molde.

"Now, brother," said the dying man,
    "Look to my children deare;
Be good unto my boy and girl,
    No friendes else have they here:

"To God and you I do commend
    My children deare this daye;
But little while be sure we have
    Within this world to staye.

"You must be father and mother both,
    And uncle all in one;
God knowes what will become of them,
    When I am dead and gone.'

5

Now, BROTHER, said the dying man, LOOK TO MY CHILDREN DEARE.

The father left his little son,
As plainlye doth appeare,
When he to perfect age should come,
Three hundred poundes a yeare.

And to his little daughter Jane
Five hundred poundes in gold,
To be paid downe on marriage-day,
Which might not be controll'd:

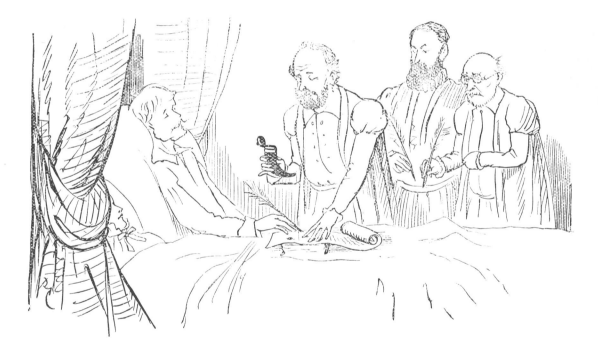

But if the children chanced to dye,
Ere they to age should come,
Their uncle should possesse their wealth;
For so the wille did run.

With that bespake their mother deare:
    "O brother kinde," quoth shee,
"You are the man must bring our babes
    To wealth or miserie:

"And if you keep them carefully,
　　Then God will you reward;
But if you otherwise should deal,
　　God will your deedes regard."

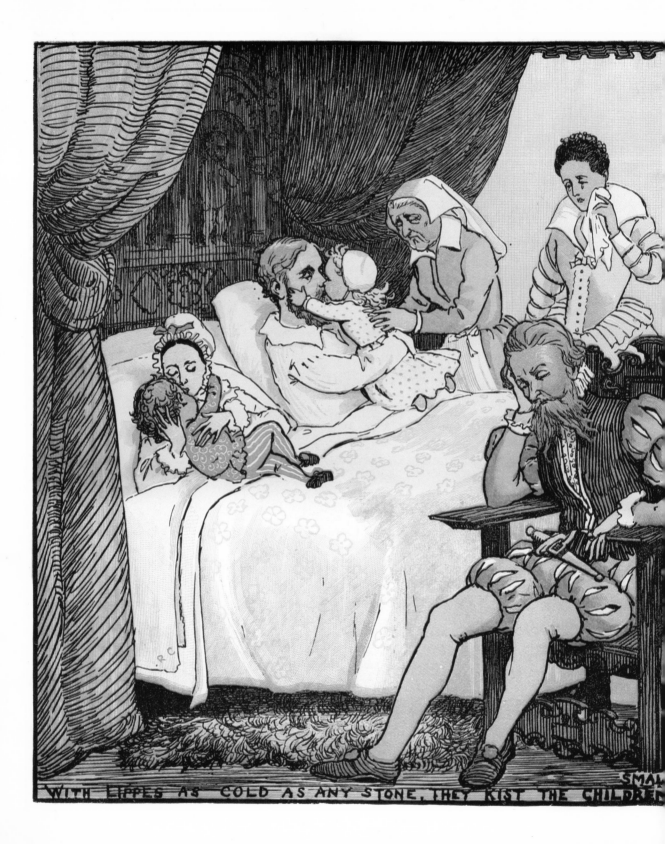

WITH LIPPES AS COLD AS ANY STONE, THEY KIST THE CHILDREN

With lippes as cold as any stone,
    They kist the children small:
"God bless you both, my children deare;"
    With that the teares did fall.

These speeches then their brother spake
    To this sicke couple there:
"The keeping of your little ones,
    Sweet sister, do not feare:

"God never prosper me nor mine,
Nor aught else that I have,
If I do wrong your chidren deare,
When you are layd in grave."

The parents being dead and gone,
  The children home he takes,
And bringes them straite unto his house,
  Where much of them he makes.

THEIR PARENTS BEING DEAD & GONE, THE CHILDREN HOME HE TAKES.

He had not kept these pretty babes
    A twelvemonth and a daye,
But, for their wealth, he did devise
    To make them both awaye.

He bargain'd with two ruffians strong,
    Which were of furious mood,
That they should take the children young,
    And slaye them in a wood.

He told his wife an artful tale,
    He would the children send
To be brought up in faire London,
    With one that was his friend.

Away then went those pretty babes,
    Rejoycing at that tide,
Rejoycing with a merry minde,
    They should on cock-horse ride.

So that the pretty speeche they had,
    Made murderers' heart relent;
And they that undertooke the deed,
    Full sore did now repent.

Yet one of them, more hard of heart,
    Did vow to do his charge,
Because the wretch, that hired him,
    Had paid him very large.

AND HE
THAT WAS OF
MILDEST
MOOD
DID SLAYE THE OTHER THERE

He took the children by the hand,
    While teares stood in their eye,
And bade them come and go with him,
    And look they did not crye:

And two long miles he ledd them on,
    While they for food complaine:
"Stay here," quoth he, "I'll bring ye bread,
    When I come back againe."

21

And when they sawe the darksome night,
They sat them downe and cryed.

Thus wandered these two prettye babes,
Till death did end their grief;
In one another's armes they dyed,
As babes wanting relief.

IN ONE ANOTHER'S ARMS THEY DYED.

No burial these prettye babes of any man receives
Till Robin-redbreast painfully did cover them with leaves.

Distributed under exclusive License in North America by Grolier
Educational Corporation.

ISBN 0-7172-9027-1
Printed in Portugal